HOW TO USE A LIGHT METER

Illuminating the Scene: A Guide to
Precise Light Measurement

Fitzpatrick J. Thompkins

Copyright © 2024 by **Fitzpatrick J. Thompkins**

All rights reserved

No part of this publication may be reproduced, stored in a retrieval system, or transmitted, in any form or by any means, electronic, mechanical, photocopying, recording, or otherwise, without the prior written permission of the author.

The information in this ebook is true and complete to the best of our knowledge. All recommendation are made without guarantee on the part of author or publisher. The author and publisher disclaim any liability in connection with the use of this information.

Table of Contents

Introduction   6
    Overview of Light Meters   9
    Importance of Correct Exposure in Photography   12
    Types of Light Meters: Incident and Reflective   14

Understanding Exposure Basics   16
    The Exposure Triangle: ISO, Aperture, and Shutter Speed   16
    How Light Meters Work   19
    Reading and Interpreting Light Meter Scales   22

Types of Light Meters   25
    Handheld Light Meters   25
    In-Camera Light Meters   28
    Smartphone Light Meter Apps   31
    Spot Meters vs. Matrix Meters   34

Setting Up Your Light Meter   37
    Calibration and Maintenance   37
    Setting ISO and Exposure Settings   40
    Customizing Metering Modes   43

Using a Handheld Light Meter   46
    Incident Light Measurement Techniques   46
    Reflective Light Measurement Techniques   49
    Measuring Flash Exposure   52

Advanced Techniques and Tips   55
    Using a Light Meter in Challenging Lighting Conditions   55

High Dynamic Range (HDR) Photography and Light Meters	58
Creative Uses of Overexposure and Underexposure	61
In-Camera Light Metering	**64**
How to Use and Interpret In-Camera Metering	64
Metering Modes: Spot, Center-Weighted, and Evaluative	67
Adjusting Exposure Compensation	69
Using Light Meters in Different Genres of Photography	**72**
Portrait Photography	72
Landscape Photography	75
Street Photography	78
Studio Photography	81
Troubleshooting Common Issues	**84**
Addressing Inaccurate Readings	84
Dealing with Low Light Conditions	87
Tips for Maintaining Your Light Meter	90
Case Studies and Practical Examples	**93**
Real-life Scenarios of Using a Light Meter	93
Comparative Analysis of Metered vs. Non-metered Photographs	96
Conclusion	**99**

Introduction

In the charming town of Eldwood, known for its captivating autumn foliage and vibrant spring blossoms, lived an aspiring photographer named Emma. Despite her passion and a keen eye for beauty, Emma often found her photos either too bright or frustratingly dim. The elusive dance of light and shadow in her photographs was a constant battle, leaving her creations a touch shy of what she envisioned.

On a crisp September morning, while Emma was meandering through a bustling flea market, a peculiar stall caught her eye. Amongst the vintage cameras and faded postcards, there lay a book titled "How to Use a Light Meter" adorned with a cover photo of the sun peeking through a dark forest canopy. Intrigued and a tad skeptical, Emma picked it up, wondering if this guide could be the answer to her photographic woes.

The vendor, a sprightly old man with a twinkle in his eye, noticed her interest. "That's not just a book," he said, his voice carrying the weight of experience, "It's a key to mastering the art of light in your photographs. It'll teach you to capture not just images, but the emotions and stories intertwined with the light that bathes them."

Emma, driven by curiosity and her unyielding desire to improve, purchased the book. That evening, nestled in her cozy reading nook, she turned its pages, each chapter a new doorway into the world of exposure, light, and shadows. The book began with the basics of light meter types—incidental and reflective—and detailed the mechanisms of each. It discussed the importance of understanding the exposure triangle: ISO, aperture, and shutter speed, which were once mere terms to Emma but now unfolded as the crucial elements of photography she had overlooked.

As autumn waned, Emma ventured outdoors, armed with her newfound knowledge and a handheld light meter she had purchased, encouraged by the book. She practiced measuring light in various settings, adjusting her camera settings as the book guided her through reflective light measurement techniques and incident light methods. With each click of her camera, Emma watched her world transform, her photos vividly echoing the beauty she saw through her lens.

Winter brought with it the challenge of low light photography, but Emma was undaunted. The book had prepared her well, offering tips on dealing with such conditions and using her light meter to gauge the subtle nuances of light, even in the dimmest environments. Her photographs of the winter solstice were nothing short of magical, capturing the serene glow of street lamps on freshly fallen snow, each flake glistening like a star against the night sky.

By spring, Emma's gallery of photographs was rich with dynamic ranges and balanced compositions. She held her first exhibition at the local community center, aptly named "Chasing Light." It was a vibrant testament to her journey from frustration to mastery, each photograph a chapter of her story, learned from the pages of her trusted guide on using a light meter.

As guests wandered through the exhibition, Emma shared her journey, recommending "How to Use a Light Meter" to budding photographers who echoed the struggles she once faced. With each recommendation, she recounted how the book not only taught her the technicalities of using a light meter but also opened her eyes to the poetic interplay of light and shadow—a dance she had learned to choreograph with precision and artistry.

The book, once a simple purchase at a flea market, had become Emma's most cherished tool, turning her once elusive dreams into a tangible reality, beautifully illuminated for the world to see.

Overview of Light Meters

Light meters are indispensable tools for photographers who want to achieve precise exposure in their images. These devices measure the intensity of light in a scene, allowing the photographer to adjust camera settings such as ISO, aperture, and shutter speed accurately to capture the scene as envisioned. There are two main types of light meters: incident and reflective, each serving a specific purpose and offering benefits under different conditions.

Incident light meters are particularly useful for measuring the amount of light falling on a subject. They do this by measuring the light that directly hits the subject, disregarding the light that the subject reflects. This method helps photographers achieve a more consistent exposure, especially in controlled environments like studios. By using an incident light meter, photographers can determine optimal exposure settings without being influenced by the subject's color or texture, which can lead to misleading readings in reflective meters.

Reflective light meters, on the other hand, measure the light bouncing off the subject and are commonly built into cameras. These meters are highly effective for field work, where conditions are variable and a photographer needs to quickly adapt to changing lighting scenarios. Reflective meters are adept at helping to evaluate the brightness of different scene elements, but they can sometimes be fooled by very dark or very light subjects, misinterpreting them as underexposed or overexposed scenes respectively.

Light meters can also differ in how they handle the spatial distribution of light. Spot meters measure light in a very small area of the frame, allowing precise measurements of specific points. This is particularly useful for high-contrast scenes where pinpointing exposure on a key element is crucial. Conversely, matrix or evaluative meters analyze the light in several zones of the frame to give a well-balanced exposure based on the overall scene, which is excellent for general shooting scenarios.

Modern photography often benefits from the integration of digital technology in light meters, which now often feature digital displays that provide a more intuitive interface and sometimes connectivity with cameras for more seamless exposure setting adjustments. Some light meters also include features for flash photography, calculating the necessary flash output to properly expose a scene, which can be a game-changer in studio settings or low-light conditions.

Ultimately, understanding and effectively utilizing a light meter can significantly enhance the technical quality of photographs. By learning to read and interpret what the light meter displays, photographers can make informed decisions about how to set their cameras for the best possible exposure. Whether shooting a dimly lit evening landscape or a brightly lit model in a studio, mastering the use of a light meter empowers photographers to capture their artistic vision with greater precision and confidence.

Importance of Correct Exposure in Photography

Correct exposure is the linchpin of great photography. It determines how light or dark an image appears and affects the clarity, mood, and detail of the photo. When photographers talk about exposure, they're referring to the amount of light that reaches the camera sensor, which is crucial for capturing images that look as close as possible to what the human eye perceives. Achieving the right exposure is a delicate balance of ISO, shutter speed, and aperture, which are the fundamental aspects of the exposure triangle.

A light meter is an invaluable tool in mastering exposure, offering a precision that the in-camera metering system might not always achieve. Cameras, although sophisticated, sometimes misinterpret scenes with high contrast or unusual lighting conditions, leading to overexposed or underexposed shots. For instance, a scene with a bright sky and a dark foreground can confuse the camera's metering system, resulting in a foreground that's too dark or a sky that's blown out. This is where a light meter steps in, providing an objective measure of the light present and how it should be captured by the camera settings.

Using a light meter involves measuring the light levels in the scene and then adjusting the camera settings based on those readings. This process helps photographers make informed decisions about the exposure settings that will best represent the scene's lighting. For photographers shooting in variable lighting conditions or aiming for consistent results in a series of shots, a light meter is essential. It becomes especially crucial in settings like studio photography, where controlling light is fundamental to achieving a specific artistic vision.

Moreover, a light meter can help photographers understand light better and improve their ability to estimate the right settings even without the meter. Regular use of a light meter trains the eye to assess lighting conditions more accurately, enhancing one's skills in manual mode and encouraging a more thoughtful approach to photography. It teaches the importance of each element of the exposure triangle and how they interact with each other, promoting a better overall understanding of photography.

Ultimately, using a light meter allows for greater artistic control. It enables photographers to execute their vision more precisely, whether they're capturing the soft glow of a sunset or the harsh lines of an urban landscape at noon. By ensuring correct exposure, photographers can avoid spending excessive time correcting their images post-production, which can often degrade image quality. In the realm of digital photography, where details matter and every pixel counts, having the right exposure from the start is invaluable. Therefore, mastering how to use a light meter is not just about technical proficiency; it's about expanding one's creative freedom in the field of photography.

Types of Light Meters: Incident and Reflective

When discussing the nuances of photography, understanding the distinct functionalities of incident and reflective light meters is crucial for achieving optimal exposure. Each type of meter offers a unique approach to measuring light, which profoundly influences the outcome of a photograph.

An incident light meter reads the light falling on the subject. It involves placing the meter near the subject and pointing it towards the camera or the primary light source. This method is highly effective because it measures the light that actually illuminates the subject, disregarding any reflections that might be coming off the subject itself. This approach helps photographers avoid underexposure or overexposure regardless of the subject's color, texture, or sheen. It's particularly useful in portraiture and other situations where accurate skin tones are critical. Photographers working in controlled lighting environments, such as studios, often rely on incident meters to ensure consistent lighting for all subjects.

Conversely, a reflective light meter measures the light reflecting off the subject and is commonly built into cameras. When using this type of meter, the device evaluates how bright the scene appears through the lens. This method is influenced heavily by the color and reflectiveness of the photographed objects; lighter colors reflect more light, leading to potential overexposure, while darker colors might be underexposed. Reflective light metering is quite versatile and especially beneficial in landscape photography, where the light varies across the scene and the photographer needs to measure specific points for accurate exposure.

Both types of meters require an understanding of their specific biases and limitations. An incident meter might not always be practical for distant subjects or expansive scenes, whereas a reflective meter might misinterpret scenes with significant contrast differences. By mastering the use of both incident and reflective light meters, photographers can adapt to various lighting conditions, ensuring that their photographs vividly capture the intended artistic or emotional impact of the scene. Understanding when and how to use each type of light meter allows photographers to greatly enhance the technical quality of their photos, making exposure a powerful tool rather than a mere setting.

Understanding Exposure Basics

The Exposure Triangle: ISO, Aperture, and Shutter Speed

Understanding the exposure triangle—comprising ISO, aperture, and shutter speed—is essential for mastering the art of photography and effectively using a light meter. Each element of the triangle interacts to affect the final exposure of an image, dictating the amount of light that reaches the camera sensor, the depth of field, and the clarity of motion.

ISO refers to the sensitivity of the camera's sensor to light. A lower ISO value, such as 100 or 200, means the sensor is less sensitive to light, which is ideal for shooting in bright conditions to avoid overexposure. Conversely, a higher ISO, such as 1600 or 3200, increases the sensor's sensitivity, making it possible to shoot in low-light conditions without necessitating a longer shutter speed or wider aperture. However, higher ISO settings can also lead to increased noise or grain in the image, potentially diminishing image quality.

Aperture is the opening within the lens through which light passes to enter the camera. Measured in f-stops, a lower value like f/1.4 indicates a wide aperture, allowing more light to enter, which decreases the depth of field and keeps the background more blurred. A higher value like f/16 indicates a smaller aperture, letting in less light, which increases the depth of field and keeps more of the image in focus. Aperture not only affects exposure but also artistic aspects of photography, such as emphasizing a subject by blurring the background (bokeh).

Shutter speed is the duration for which the camera shutter is open to expose light onto the camera sensor. Faster shutter speeds like 1/1000 second are crucial for freezing motion, such as capturing a bird in flight, and require more light or higher ISO settings to achieve correct exposure. Slower shutter speeds like 1 second allow more light to reach the sensor, suitable for low-light conditions or creating effects like the blur of moving water.

A light meter assists photographers in balancing these settings by providing a reading that indicates how adjustments to ISO, aperture, and shutter speed will affect exposure. By using a light meter, photographers can determine the best combination of exposure settings to achieve the desired photographic effect, whether that's a bright and clear photo under harsh sunlight or a moody, dimly lit scene with just enough detail.

For instance, in a landscape scene with varied lighting, a photographer might use a light meter to decide on an initial aperture setting that provides the desired depth of field, then adjust the ISO and shutter speed accordingly to ensure the exposure is neither too bright nor too dark. In portrait photography under studio lighting, the light meter can help set the aperture to control the depth of field and adjust the lights and camera settings to ensure the subject is perfectly illuminated.

The exposure triangle and the light meter together provide a foundation for making informed decisions about how a photograph will look. Understanding how to balance ISO, aperture, and shutter speed helps photographers not only to control the technical aspects of exposure but also to enhance their creative control over their images.

How Light Meters Work

Understanding how light meters work is essential for mastering the art of photography, as they are fundamental tools for achieving perfect exposure. Light meters evaluate the intensity of light in a scene and suggest the optimal settings for aperture, shutter speed, and ISO to ensure that photographs are exposed correctly. This process is crucial for both amateur and professional photographers aiming to capture images that are neither too dark nor overly bright.

At the core of a light meter's functionality is its ability to measure the amount of light. Light meters contain a photosensitive component, typically a photodiode, which converts light into an electrical charge. This charge is then measured, and the meter calculates the exposure settings based on the sensitivity of the film or sensor (ISO), the aperture size, and the shutter speed. This calculation is guided by a fundamental principle of photography—the inverse square law, which states that the intensity of light radiating from a source inversely decreases exponentially with the square of the distance from the source.

When a photographer adjusts their camera settings based on a light meter's readings, they are aligning their exposure to the "middle gray" or 18% gray reference. This standard assumes that every scene naturally averages to this tone, which is a midway point between absolute black and pure white. This reference is critical because it helps maintain consistency in exposure across different lighting conditions. However, it's important to note that this assumption doesn't always hold true in high contrast or unusually lit environments. In such cases, photographers must use their judgment to adjust exposure settings beyond what the light meter suggests, to capture details in very bright or dark areas.

Modern digital cameras often have built-in light meters which typically operate in one of three modes: spot, center-weighted, and evaluative (or matrix) metering. Spot metering measures light in a small area of the frame, center-weighted takes an average reading from the middle of the frame, and evaluative metering analyzes the light in several zones of the frame to achieve a balanced exposure. Each mode has its advantages and is suited to different photographic conditions. Spot metering is ideal for scenes where the subject is significantly brighter or darker than the background. Center-weighted metering benefits portraits where the subject is centrally placed, and evaluative metering works well for evenly exposed shots across diverse lighting scenarios.

Additionally, most light meters allow photographers to choose between incident and reflective metering, as previously discussed. Understanding the difference between these measuring methods and when to use each is crucial for controlling the quality and mood of the final image.

In essence, the workings of a light meter are central to understanding exposure in photography. By measuring light accurately and interpreting a light meter's readings correctly, photographers can greatly enhance their ability to capture images that are visually compelling and technically sound. This foundational knowledge not only improves a photographer's skill set but also expands their creative possibilities in capturing light and shadow.

Reading and Interpreting Light Meter Scales

Mastering the use of a light meter involves understanding how to read and interpret its scales effectively. Light meters, whether digital or analog, provide essential data that helps photographers make informed decisions about exposure settings. Grasping this concept is a fundamental skill in achieving consistently well-exposed images.

A light meter primarily measures the intensity of light and represents this measurement through various scales and units, the most common being the EV (Exposure Value) system or a direct numerical representation corresponding to specific camera settings like aperture and shutter speed. In the realm of digital light meters, readings are typically displayed on an LCD screen, providing immediate feedback in a numeric format. These meters calculate the optimal exposure based on the light measurement and the ISO setting inputted by the user, offering recommended settings for aperture and shutter speed.

In contrast, analog light meters, often seen in older camera models or handheld devices, use a needle or dial system to display the measurement. The user must align the needle with a corresponding marker or set of markers that indicate the correct exposure based on the current ISO setting and prevailing light conditions. This system requires a bit more interpretation as it's manual, but it still follows the basic principles of light measurement.

Interpreting these scales begins by setting the light meter to the appropriate ISO, which should match the camera's ISO setting. The meter will then provide a reading based on the captured light. In digital meters, the display may show a straightforward number or a series of numbers indicating suitable combinations of aperture and shutter speed for achieving a balanced exposure. For instance, a reading might indicate f/4 at 1/250th of a second, suggesting these settings will result in a well-exposed shot for the given lighting conditions and ISO.

In the case of analog meters, interpreting the scale often involves aligning a movable dial—based on the meter reading—with a fixed index mark to reveal possible combinations of aperture and shutter speed that would yield proper exposure. This might seem less direct compared to digital meters, but it offers photographers a tactile sense of control over the exposure process, allowing for adjustments based on personal preference or creative intent.

Moreover, understanding the zone system can enhance the use of light meter scales, especially for analog meters. The zone system divides the tonal range into zones from pure black to pure white, helping photographers visualize how light and dark areas of the scene will appear in the final image based on the meter readings. For example, placing a subject's skin tones in Zone VI allows for detail preservation in both highlights and shadows, depending on the lighting scenario.

Effective use of light meter scales is not just about reading numbers or aligning needles; it's about interpreting these readings to suit the specific photographic situation. Whether adjusting for backlit subjects or compensating for reflective surfaces, photographers must apply their understanding of light meter scales to control the interplay of light and shadow in their images, ensuring every shot is exposed just as intended. This mastery forms a cornerstone of skilled photography, transforming technical knowledge into artistic expression.

Types of Light Meters

Handheld Light Meters

Handheld light meters are an essential tool for photographers who need precise control over their exposure settings, providing accuracy that in-camera meters may not offer, especially in complex lighting conditions. These devices are designed to be portable and easy to use, offering the ability to measure ambient light and flash lighting independently of the camera's built-in metering system.

The primary advantage of using a handheld light meter is its ability to measure light more accurately. Unlike camera meters that measure reflected light, handheld light meters typically measure incident light, which does not depend on the subject's reflectance. This is particularly useful in high-contrast scenes where in-camera meters might be misled by bright or dark areas within the frame. For example, photographing a model in a white dress against a dark background can trick a camera's reflective meter into underexposing the scene, whereas a handheld light meter will measure the light falling on the subject, ensuring the dress and model are exposed correctly.

Many handheld meters also offer spot metering capabilities, allowing photographers to take precise readings from distant subjects. This is especially valuable in landscape photography, where lighting across the scene can vary significantly. Spot metering helps determine the exposure for a particular area of the frame without being influenced by other elements in the scene that might have different lighting.

Moreover, handheld light meters are indispensable for studio photography. They enable photographers to establish and control lighting ratios between multiple light sources, ensuring that each light contributes correctly to the exposure. By taking readings from different areas of the set, photographers can adjust their lights to achieve the desired effect, whether that's ensuring even lighting across a group or highlighting a single subject in a dramatic style.

Another feature of handheld light meters is the ability to measure flash exposure. This is crucial in studio settings or when using fill flash in outdoor photography. The meter can calculate the necessary settings for the flash to ensure it integrates seamlessly with the ambient light, providing natural-looking results that camera meters might not achieve on their own.

For photographers working with film, especially those using large format or non-metered cameras, a handheld light meter is nearly indispensable. It becomes the primary method for determining exposure, as many film cameras lack the sophisticated metering systems found in modern digital cameras.

In addition to their technical capabilities, handheld light meters are also valued for their educational role. They force photographers to think more critically about light, exposure, and the photographic process, enhancing their skills and understanding of photography. Learning to use a handheld light meter involves understanding how light behaves and how different settings on the meter affect the reading it produces, which can significantly improve a photographer's ability to visualize and plan a shot before pressing the shutter.

In conclusion, handheld light meters offer a robust, reliable solution for managing exposure in photography. By providing precise measurements of incident and flash light, they allow photographers to create consistent, well-exposed images across a wide range of settings. Their use encourages a deeper engagement with the technical aspects of photography, leading to better outcomes and a more comprehensive understanding of the art and science of photography.

In-Camera Light Meters

In-camera light meters are essential tools embedded within digital cameras that play a critical role in measuring the intensity of light in a scene to determine the optimal exposure settings. These meters have evolved significantly over the years and are integral to both amateur and professional photography, ensuring that the camera can automatically adjust its settings for the best possible shot.

The primary function of an in-camera light meter is to evaluate the light that passes through the lens (TTL) and reflect off the scene, offering photographers a reliable guide to setting their exposure. This type of metering considers the brightness of various parts of the frame and provides recommendations on shutter speed, aperture, and ISO to achieve a balanced exposure.

There are three main types of metering modes commonly found in modern digital cameras: spot, center-weighted, and evaluative (also known as matrix or multi-segment metering). Each mode has a unique way of reading light and offers distinct advantages depending on the shooting conditions and the photographer's intent.

Spot metering measures light from a very small area of the frame, typically around 1-5% of the viewfinder area. This precision allows photographers to expose for a subject's key detail, such as the face in portraiture or a specific object in a complex, high-contrast environment. It is especially useful in scenes where the background is significantly brighter or darker than the subject.

Center-weighted metering evaluates the light in the middle of the frame and its immediate surroundings, assigning greater importance to the central part of the image. This method is a bit of a throwback to older analog cameras but remains popular for its predictability and effectiveness, particularly in traditional portraiture where the subject is centrally placed.

Evaluative metering, known in some camera systems as matrix or multi-segment metering, is the most complex form of light metering used in modern cameras. It divides the frame into multiple zones, which are analyzed on color, luminance, and focus in conjunction to the active autofocus points. The camera then compares these readings to in-built databases of images to calculate the best overall exposure. This mode is highly adaptive and works exceptionally well in dynamic and unpredictably lit conditions, providing balanced exposures even in challenging light scenarios.

Learning to use in-camera light meters effectively requires an understanding of these modes and when to deploy them based on the lighting conditions and the artistic goals of the photograph. For instance, spot metering can be indispensable for capturing wildlife details against a complex backdrop, while evaluative metering can effortlessly handle the rapid lighting changes during a sunset landscape shoot.

Moreover, understanding the biases of in-camera light meters, such as their tendency to interpret scenes based on middle gray (a concept known as the 18% gray rule), can help photographers make necessary manual adjustments. Adjusting exposure compensation is a critical skill when dealing with scenes that are predominantly brighter or darker than middle gray, as it allows the photographer to override the camera's automatic settings to capture true-to-life exposure.

In sum, mastering in-camera light meters involves not just knowing what each metering mode does, but also when to use them and how to adjust their recommendations to suit specific photographic needs. This ensures that photographers can rely on their equipment to faithfully capture their artistic vision, regardless of the complexity of the lighting environment.

Smartphone Light Meter Apps

In the realm of photography, the evolution of technology has extended the functionality of traditional devices to smartphones, including the use of light meters through various apps. Smartphone light meter apps are a modern solution for photographers who prefer a more accessible and portable way to measure light without carrying additional equipment. These apps utilize the phone's built-in camera or ambient light sensor to approximate light readings, offering a convenient alternative to traditional handheld light meters.

Smartphone light meter apps work by using the camera to assess the brightness of the scene photographed. Some apps may also use the device's ambient light sensor, although this is less common. The apps analyze the light information and then calculate the optimal exposure settings based on the user's input regarding ISO, aperture, and desired shutter speed. Users can typically adjust these settings manually within the app to see how changes affect the suggested exposure, making it a dynamic tool for learning and understanding exposure variations.

The accuracy of smartphone light meter apps can vary. While they are generally reliable in consistent lighting conditions, their performance may diminish in more complex lighting scenarios such as backlit environments or scenes with high dynamic range. This variation is partly because smartphone sensors are less sophisticated compared to dedicated light meters, and the apps rely heavily on software algorithms that interpret the sensor data. However, for amateur photographers or those learning the basics of light measurement, these apps serve as an excellent educational tool and starting point.

There are several popular light meter apps available on the market, each offering different features. Some apps are designed to mimic professional light meters closely, providing detailed readings and multiple metering modes such as spot, matrix, or center-weighted measurements. Other apps might include additional photography tools like depth of field calculators, exposure compensation tutorials, and even color temperature estimators.

When using smartphone light meter apps, it's essential to calibrate the app if possible. Calibration involves adjusting the app's settings based on a known reference light source or a professional-grade light meter's reading to enhance accuracy. Furthermore, users should be aware of their specific app's limitations and strengths, experimenting within various conditions to get a feel for when the app's readings are most reliable.

In conclusion, smartphone light meter apps represent a fusion of traditional photography techniques with contemporary technology, making light measurement more accessible to a broader audience. They are particularly useful for hobbyists, photography students, and professionals looking for a lightweight backup tool. While they may not entirely replace professional handheld meters in terms of precision, these apps are a valuable addition to a photographer's toolkit, especially in informal or impromptu shooting situations where carrying minimal gear is advantageous.

Spot Meters vs. Matrix Meters

Spot meters and matrix meters represent two advanced types of light meters, each offering unique benefits and challenges in measuring light for photography. Understanding the difference between these two can significantly enhance a photographer's ability to capture images with the desired exposure.

Spot meters are highly precise instruments that measure light in a very small area of the frame, typically about 1% to 5% of the total viewfinder area. This allows photographers to target specific elements in a scene, making spot meters ideal for high-contrast situations where light varies significantly across the scene. For instance, in landscape photography, a spot meter can be used to measure the light on a brightly lit cloud or a shadowed rock, enabling the photographer to make exposure decisions based on the most important element of the composition. This type of metering is invaluable for achieving correct exposure in scenes where the subject is backlit or under unusual lighting that could confuse more general metering methods.

Matrix meters, also known as evaluative or multi-segment meters, are more complex and are typically built into modern digital cameras. These meters evaluate the light in multiple zones of the frame, which can range from a handful to several hundred depending on the camera's design. The camera then uses a sophisticated algorithm to determine the overall exposure. This algorithm takes into account not only the light in each zone but also factors like the location of focus points, color, and sometimes even the distance to the subject as provided by the autofocus system. Matrix metering is incredibly versatile and generally provides excellent results in most common photography scenarios, especially where the light distribution is even, or the scene doesn't contain extreme contrasts.

The choice between using a spot meter and a matrix meter often depends on the photographer's specific needs and the complexity of the lighting in the scene. Spot metering requires a more hands-on approach, often preferred by professional photographers who demand precise control over every aspect of their exposure. It's particularly useful for fine art photography, dramatic landscapes, and any situation where the light on the subject differs significantly from its surroundings.

Matrix metering, on the other hand, offers great convenience and efficiency, making it suitable for beginners and professionals alike, especially in fast-paced environments like event photography or photojournalism where conditions change rapidly and there isn't always time to make nuanced adjustments based on spot readings.

In essence, understanding when to use spot metering versus matrix metering is a key skill in a photographer's arsenal, allowing them to adapt quickly to different lighting conditions and capture images with more accurate exposure. By mastering these tools, photographers can ensure that their images not only capture scenes as seen but also as envisioned, using light not just as a necessity but as an artistic ally.

Setting Up Your Light Meter

Calibration and Maintenance

Calibrating and maintaining a light meter are critical steps to ensure its accuracy and reliability over time. A properly calibrated light meter guarantees that photographers can trust the exposure readings it provides, essential for producing consistently high-quality photographs. Regular maintenance also prolongs the life of the equipment, protecting the investment made in purchasing a high-quality meter.

The calibration of a light meter should be approached systematically. For digital meters, calibration often involves comparing the device's readings with a known light source or a standard reflective object under controlled conditions. Many modern digital light meters come with built-in calibration controls that guide users through the process. This typically involves setting the meter to a specific mode where it reads a standardized light output and automatically adjusts its settings to match the expected values. This feature is invaluable because it simplifies what could otherwise be a complex and technical process.

For analog light meters, calibration might require manual adjustments. This could involve turning a screw or dial on the meter itself to align the needle with a specific mark when exposed to a predetermined light level. For those who are not comfortable performing these adjustments themselves, professional calibration services are available and might be a preferable option, especially for high-end equipment used in professional settings.

Maintenance of light meters, both digital and analog, includes regular cleaning and careful storage. The light sensor, particularly, should be kept clean and clear of dust, dirt, and fingerprints, as these can affect its sensitivity and accuracy. It's advised to use a soft, dry cloth to gently wipe the sensor. Avoid using chemical cleaners unless they are specified safe by the manufacturer, as harsh substances can damage the sensor's surface.

The body of the light meter should also be cleaned regularly to prevent build-up of grime that could eventually interfere with the buttons or dials. For analog meters, it is essential to ensure that any moving parts remain functional and are not hindered by dust or rust. Storing the meter in a dry, cool place is recommended to avoid exposure to moisture and extreme temperatures, which can affect the meter's functionality and lead to deterioration over time.

Batteries should be checked and replaced as needed. It is important not to leave exhausted batteries inside the meter for extended periods, as they can leak and cause damage. For meters used infrequently, removing the batteries when the device is stored can prevent unexpected battery leaks.

Finally, regular testing against a known light source or standard can help detect any drift in the meter's accuracy that might develop over time. Conducting such tests periodically ensures that any degradation in performance is caught and addressed promptly, maintaining the reliability of the meter's readings.

By adhering to these calibration and maintenance practices, photographers ensure that their light meter remains a trusted tool in their photography toolkit, enabling them to capture perfectly exposed images consistently. This diligence not only enhances the quality of their work but also contributes to the longevity and dependability of their equipment.

Setting ISO and Exposure Settings

Setting ISO and exposure settings correctly is an essential skill for photographers aiming to use a light meter effectively. ISO, one of the primary elements of the exposure triangle along with shutter speed and aperture, affects the camera sensor's sensitivity to light. Properly configuring these settings is crucial for leveraging a light meter to capture well-exposed photographs.

ISO setting is the starting point in configuring exposure settings when using a light meter. It determines how sensitive the camera is to incoming light. A lower ISO, such as 100 or 200, is ideal for shooting in bright conditions without introducing noise, which can degrade the image quality. Conversely, in low-light conditions, a higher ISO, such as 1600 or 3200, might be necessary to capture images without motion blur. However, increasing ISO can lead to more noise. Thus, the choice of ISO must balance the need for exposure against the desire for the least amount of noise.

Once ISO is set, a light meter helps determine the correct shutter speed and aperture settings based on the light measurement and the chosen ISO. For instance, if a light meter reading suggests that there is too much or too little light hitting the subject, adjustments can be made to the aperture or shutter speed to compensate. The aperture controls the amount of light entering through the lens by enlarging or reducing the size of the lens opening. A larger aperture (a lower f-number, like f/2.8) allows more light to enter, which is useful in darker situations. In contrast, a smaller aperture (a higher f-number, like f/16) restricts light, ideal for very bright conditions.

Shutter speed, on the other hand, determines how long the camera's sensor is exposed to light. A faster shutter speed (like 1/1000 second) lets in less light and is good for freezing motion, while a slower shutter speed (like 1 second) allows more light to hit the sensor, useful for low-light conditions or achieving a motion blur effect for dynamic images.

The process of setting up a light meter involves first taking a reading of the current lighting conditions. The meter will then display the settings needed to achieve a balanced exposure based on the initial ISO setting. If the suggested settings do not align with the creative vision or practical requirements of the shoot, such as maintaining a specific depth of field or motion effect, the photographer can alter the ISO or modify the aperture and shutter speed while observing changes in the light meter's readings.

Moreover, many modern light meters allow for these variables to be adjusted within the device itself, enabling the photographer to see hypothetical outcomes before changing the settings on the camera. This feature is particularly beneficial in teaching new photographers the immediate impact of exposure changes, thereby deepening their understanding of photographic exposure.

Ultimately, mastering the interaction between ISO, aperture, and shutter speed, with the aid of a light meter, is fundamental for photographers to control the artistic and technical qualities of their images. This knowledge ensures that regardless of the lighting conditions, the photographer can make informed decisions to produce consistently well-exposed photos.

Customizing Metering Modes

Customizing metering modes on a light meter is an essential skill for photographers who want to tailor their exposure settings to specific shooting conditions. This customization allows for greater control over the resulting image by adjusting how the camera or light meter interprets the light in a given scene.

Metering modes determine how much of the frame the camera considers when calculating the correct exposure. Each mode is designed to handle different lighting situations and subject compositions. The most common metering modes available in modern cameras and some sophisticated light meters include spot, center-weighted, and evaluative (also known as matrix or multi-segment) metering.

Spot metering is highly precise and measures only a small area of the entire frame, usually around 1-5% of the viewfinder area. This mode is perfect for photographs where the subject is backlit or when there are significant differences in brightness within the scene. By isolating a small area, photographers can ensure that a crucial element of the image, such as a face in portrait photography, is correctly exposed, regardless of the rest of the scene's lighting.

Center-weighted metering takes into account a larger area than spot metering, focusing primarily on the center of the frame and gradually considering less light towards the edges. This mode is useful for scenes where the subject is centrally located and the background lighting is not dramatically different. It's particularly favored for traditional portrait shots where the background is uniform and doesn't require as much attention in exposure.

Evaluative metering, the most complex of the three, evaluates the light in multiple zones across the entire frame and then combines this data to calculate the best overall exposure. Modern cameras typically use advanced algorithms to analyze each segment, considering factors like distance, color, and luminance to make a more balanced exposure decision. This mode is incredibly versatile and suitable for most situations, especially in highly dynamic environments where light conditions are constantly changing, such as in sports or wildlife photography.

Learning to customize these metering modes according to the specific needs of a shoot can dramatically enhance the quality of photographs. Photographers should practice with each setting to understand how it affects their images under various conditions. For instance, experimenting with spot metering in harshly lit conditions can reveal details that would otherwise be lost in shadow or highlight if a different metering mode were used.

Additionally, many advanced cameras and meters allow for further customization of these modes. For example, some cameras enable the adjustment of the size of the area affected by spot or center-weighted metering, and others offer hybrid modes that combine the principles of two different metering modes to suit specific needs.

By mastering the customization of metering modes, photographers not only gain more control over their equipment but also deepen their understanding of how light interacts with their subjects. This knowledge is crucial for making informed decisions in the field and for achieving consistently well-exposed images across a wide range of shooting scenarios.

Using a Handheld Light Meter

Incident Light Measurement Techniques

Using a handheld light meter for incident light measurement is a technique that offers photographers precision and control in determining exposure. This method involves measuring the light that falls directly on the subject, rather than the light reflected from it. It is particularly effective in providing accurate exposure readings that are not influenced by the color or texture of the subject, which can often mislead in-camera reflective meters.

To start using a handheld light meter for incident light measurement, the first step is to set the meter to the correct measurement mode. Most handheld light meters have a switch or a menu option that allows you to choose between incident and reflective metering. Once the incident light mode is selected, you will typically use a white dome or diffuser that covers the light sensor. This dome helps to capture all the light falling on the subject from the scene, providing a comprehensive measurement.

Next, position the light meter at the location of the subject. It's crucial to hold the meter so that the white dome is facing the direction of the camera or the primary light source. This orientation ensures that the meter accurately reads the intensity of light that the subject is actually receiving. If photographing a person, for example, the meter should be held at their face level, with the dome directed towards the camera or the primary light source.

Adjust the meter to the camera's ISO setting. Most handheld light meters allow you to input the ISO sensitivity of the camera being used. This setting is vital as it ensures the light meter's sensitivity matches that of the camera, providing a reading that accurately reflects the exposure needed for the given ISO.

Once the meter is in position and set up, activate the meter to take a reading. This usually involves pressing a button on the meter. The meter will then display the appropriate aperture and shutter speed settings required to achieve an optimal exposure under the existing lighting conditions. These readings should be manually entered into the camera. Some meters also provide EV (exposure value) readings, which can be particularly useful if working with manual exposure cameras or when wanting to maintain consistent exposure across different shots.

When using the meter in changing light conditions, it's important to take multiple readings as lighting conditions change, especially in dynamic environments like outdoor settings where clouds may intermittently cover the sun. Consistent checking ensures that the exposure is always set right, regardless of shifts in natural light.

Incident light measurement with a handheld light meter also enables creative control over the image. By understanding the amount of light actually reaching the subject, photographers can make informed decisions about whether to adjust the light itself—perhaps by adding diffusion material to soften harsh sunlight—or by modifying the camera settings to achieve a specific artistic effect, such as deliberately overexposing to create a high-key portrait.

Overall, mastering incident light measurement techniques with a handheld light meter empowers photographers to capture images with precise exposure, tailored to the unique requirements of each shooting scenario. This method not only ensures technically sound photographs but also supports the photographer's vision by allowing adjustments based on the actual light environment, leading to consistently better results.

Reflective Light Measurement Techniques

Reflective light measurement techniques using a handheld light meter are integral to photography, enabling photographers to precisely determine the exposure based on how light reflects off the subject and its surroundings. Unlike incident light measurement, which captures the light falling directly onto the subject, reflective techniques assess the intensity of light after it has bounced off the subject, which is crucial for accurate exposure settings in diverse photographic conditions.

To effectively use a handheld light meter for reflective measurements, one must first ensure the meter is set to the reflective mode. This setup is typically marked distinctly on the meter and is necessary because the device needs to interpret the light entering through its lens, similar to how a camera views a scene.

The basic procedure involves pointing the light meter's sensor towards the subject from the position of the camera. The meter then evaluates the light reflected from the subject. It's essential to be mindful of the angle at which the meter is held, as different angles can capture different amounts of light, leading to variations in exposure settings. An optimal practice is to aim the meter directly at the center of the composition or the area that the photographer wants to be optimally exposed.

Reflective light meters are especially proficient at handling complex lighting situations. For example, in a scene with significant backlighting, where a subject might appear as a silhouette, a reflective meter can help assess the light intensity of the background, allowing photographers to adjust their camera settings to capture detail in the brighter parts of the scene. This technique is invaluable for maintaining the texture and detail in bright areas, which might otherwise be lost.

Moreover, when working in environments with contrasting light conditions—such as a landscape with deep shadows and bright skies—photographers can use a reflective meter to take multiple readings: one for the shadows and one for the highlights. These readings can then guide the photographer in choosing a balanced exposure that preserves details across the scene, a technique often referred to as "exposure bracketing."

Advanced use of a reflective handheld light meter often involves understanding the zone system, a method developed by Ansel Adams and Fred Archer. This system divides the tonal range into zones from pure black to pure white and helps photographers decide how light or dark a scene should appear based on the metering data collected. By measuring the light of different elements within the frame, photographers can assign these elements to specific zones, thus gaining more control over the final image's tonal qualities.

Finally, reflective measurement demands awareness of the meter's calibration and sensitivity to different colors and brightness levels. Since reflective meters can be influenced by the color and sheen of the subject, photographers must sometimes adjust the recommended exposure settings to compensate for these factors. This might mean slightly overexposing a scene with predominantly dark tones or underexposing a scene with lots of bright, reflective surfaces.

Mastering reflective light measurement with a handheld light meter requires practice and experience, as the interpretation of readings can be subjective and situation-dependent. However, developing proficiency in this technique allows photographers to capture images that are technically sound and artistically fulfilling, with exposure levels that are true to the photographer's vision.

Measuring Flash Exposure

Measuring flash exposure with a handheld light meter is a critical skill for photographers who want to control lighting precisely, particularly in studio settings or during indoor events. Understanding how to effectively use a handheld light meter for flash photography ensures that the images are neither overexposed nor underexposed, capturing the essence of the subject with the desired lighting effect.

The process begins by setting the handheld light meter to the flash mode, often indicated as a lightning bolt symbol or simply labeled "flash." This mode is specifically designed to measure the burst of light produced by a flash unit, rather than continuous light. The photographer then enters the camera's ISO setting and the desired aperture into the meter. These settings should match what the photographer plans to use for the shot, as they significantly influence the exposure calculation.

Next, the placement of the light meter is crucial. Unlike ambient light measurements, the meter should be positioned where the subject will be, directed back toward the camera or the primary flash unit. This orientation ensures that the meter captures the light as it falls on the subject, providing a reading that represents the exposure the subject will receive.

Once the meter is in place, the photographer triggers the flash manually or uses a wireless trigger that synchronizes with the meter. The burst of light from the flash is then captured by the light meter, which calculates the amount of light and subsequently displays the correct shutter speed to use for the given ISO and aperture settings. This reading is critical as it tells the photographer exactly how long the camera's sensor needs to be exposed to the light to achieve a proper exposure.

In situations involving multiple flash units or complex lighting setups, a photographer may need to take multiple readings. Each flash unit should be tested individually, with the light meter placed in the same position each time to ensure consistency. The readings from each flash are then combined to determine the overall exposure settings. Some advanced light meters can handle measurements from multiple flashes simultaneously, providing a cumulative exposure value that accounts for all the light sources.

It's also important to consider the sync speed of the camera when working with flash. The sync speed is the fastest shutter speed at which the camera can fire while completely exposing the sensor to the flash. Exceeding this speed can result in images that are only partially illuminated. The light meter's suggested shutter speed should always be at or below the camera's sync speed unless using high-speed sync techniques.

Using a handheld light meter to measure flash exposure not only helps in achieving technically accurate photographs but also allows for creative control over lighting effects. Photographers can experiment with different flash intensities and positions, immediately seeing the impact of changes through the meter's readings and adjusting accordingly. This method of measuring flash exposure empowers photographers to take full advantage of flash photography's potential, leading to beautifully lit, dynamic images that might otherwise be difficult to achieve through camera-only settings or guesswork.

Advanced Techniques and Tips

Using a Light Meter in Challenging Lighting Conditions

Using a light meter effectively in challenging lighting conditions requires a deep understanding of both the environment and the equipment. Challenging lighting can include scenarios with extreme contrast, low light, backlighting, and highly reflective surfaces. Mastering the use of a light meter in these situations can drastically improve the quality of the photographs.

In environments with extreme contrast, such as bright sunlight mixed with deep shadows, the dynamic range of the camera may be insufficient to capture details in both the highlights and the shadows. Here, a light meter becomes invaluable. By taking readings from both the brightest and darkest areas, you can determine an exposure that preserves detail across the scene. For instance, you might set your exposure to retain highlight detail and then use fill light or reflectors to brighten the shadows, based on what your light meter tells you.

Low light conditions present another challenge, often resulting in grainy photos or blurry movements. Using a light meter, adjust the ISO setting as low as possible while still achieving an exposure that doesn't sacrifice shutter speed or aperture beyond acceptable limits. In such settings, an incident light meter can be particularly helpful because it measures the light falling on the subject directly, enabling more accurate adjustments than the camera's built-in reflective meter.

Backlighting occurs when the main light source is behind the subject, causing the subject to appear dark and underexposed when using standard metering techniques. To counter this, point an incident light meter back towards the direction from where the camera will be shooting to measure the light falling on the subject, not the light coming from behind it. This approach ensures the subject is correctly exposed, regardless of the strong light in the background.

Highly reflective surfaces, like metal or water, can trick a reflective light meter into underexposing the entire scene. The light meter interprets the bright reflection as an overall bright scene, leading to darker images. To manage this, switch to manual mode and use an incident meter to measure the light around the subject, not the light reflecting directly into the lens. Alternatively, if only using a reflective meter, compensate by adjusting the exposure manually to counteract the meter's tendency to underexpose the shot.

In addition to these techniques, there are a few tips that can enhance light meter usage in tough lighting:

1. **Use the histogram on your camera along with the light meter readings**. The histogram provides a visual representation of the exposure levels across the image and can help confirm whether the light meter's readings are leading to the best possible exposure.

2. **Bracket your exposures**. Especially in highly variable lighting, take multiple shots at different exposure settings (exposure bracketing) to ensure you capture a usable image. This can be crucial in environments where lighting conditions change rapidly, such as during sunrise or sunset.

3. **Regularly calibrate your light meter**. Ensure that your light meter is calibrated and functioning accurately, particularly if you often shoot in challenging conditions. A misreading due to calibration issues can exacerbate difficulties with exposure in complex lighting environments.

By integrating these advanced techniques and tips into your photography practice, you can leverage a light meter to overcome challenging lighting conditions, ensuring high-quality captures even in the most difficult environments. This not only enhances your technical skillset but also expands your creative possibilities.

High Dynamic Range (HDR) Photography and Light Meters

High Dynamic Range (HDR) photography is a technique used to enhance the dynamic range of an image—the contrast between the darkest and lightest tones. HDR allows photographers to capture details in both the highlights and shadows that would otherwise be lost due to the limitations of the camera sensor. Using a light meter effectively in HDR photography is essential to achieving the best results, as it involves taking multiple exposures of the same scene at different brightness levels and then blending them together.

To begin with HDR photography, understanding how to measure light for each exposure is key. Typically, HDR requires at least three shots taken at different exposures: one at the camera's base exposure, another underexposed, and a third that is overexposed. Using a light meter accurately can dictate the success of these shots. An incident light meter is particularly useful in this context because it measures the light falling on the scene directly, providing a baseline reading that is not influenced by the reflectiveness of the subject or background.

The process starts by taking a reading with the light meter to determine the base exposure of the scene. This setting is considered the 'normal' exposure, where mid-tones are well balanced. The next step is to adjust the exposure value (EV) to capture additional frames. For the underexposed frame, decrease the exposure by setting the camera to capture darker areas of the scene, which preserves details in the highlights. Conversely, increase the exposure for the overexposed frame to capture details in the shadows. Adjustments are usually made in increments of 1-2 EV steps. The precise amount of adjustment can vary based on the scene's lighting and the dynamic range of the camera used.

It's important to note that while reflective light meters, typically found in cameras, can also be used for HDR, they might not always provide the best results in high contrast situations. They often meter based on the brightness of the subjects, which can be deceptive if the scene has very bright or very dark areas. Therefore, using an incident light meter helps in getting more accurate readings by ignoring the variations in subject reflectance.

After capturing the required exposures, the next phase is blending these images into a single HDR image. This is usually done through post-processing software that can merge these exposures, adjusting for the best parts of each according to the light data captured. The software aligns the images, blends them, and applies tone-mapping techniques to create a single image that reveals greater details across the entire tonal range.

A few tips for mastering HDR with light meters include:
- Always use a tripod to ensure that images are perfectly aligned and sharp.

- If possible, shoot in RAW format to retain maximum details and allow for more effective post-processing.
- Test different exposure brackets to find the best range for your specific scene and lighting conditions.
- Be mindful of moving subjects as they can create ghosting effects in the final HDR image.

Incorporating HDR techniques into photography not only enhances the visual impact of images but also expands the creative possibilities. By effectively utilizing a light meter to gauge and adjust exposures accurately, photographers can achieve high-quality HDR images that showcase vivid details and stunning contrasts.

Creative Uses of Overexposure and Underexposure

Overexposure and underexposure, typically avoided in traditional photography, can be wielded creatively to produce unique and compelling images. By intentionally manipulating exposure settings with the help of a light meter, photographers can accentuate mood, emphasize details, or convey a particular artistic vision. Here's how a deep understanding of light meter usage enhances the creative application of these techniques.

Creative Uses of Overexposure

Overexposure involves allowing more light into the camera than the standard settings suggest, resulting in brighter images where details may be washed out. This technique can be particularly effective in creating high-key photographs that exude a light, airy, and ethereal quality. High-key photography is often used in fashion and portrait shots to convey purity and simplicity.

Another creative use of overexposure is to deliberately obscure specific details of a subject to draw attention to others or create a sense of mystery. For example, overexposing the background can help in isolating the subject from its surroundings, making the subject appear more prominent and focused. This technique is also useful in conveying a sense of depth or highlighting form and color over texture.

Photographers can use a light meter to measure the key light accurately and then manually adjust the exposure settings to increase brightness, carefully controlling the extent of overexposure to maintain a balance between the artistic effect and retaining essential details.

Creative Uses of Underexposure

Underexposure, conversely, involves limiting the amount of light captured by the camera, creating a darker image with enriched colors and enhanced textures. This technique is useful in adding drama and mood to a scene. For instance, underexposing a sunset can intensify the colors in the sky and the silhouettes in the landscape, producing a more dramatic and impactful image.

In genres like horror or thriller, underexposure can play a crucial role in setting the tone. Darker images can evoke feelings of fear, uncertainty, and suspense. Photographers can achieve this by using their light meter to determine the optimal exposure and then deliberately dialing back the exposure to deepen shadows and obscure details, enhancing the ominous feel of the image.

Underexposure can also be employed to draw attention to specific areas of light within a mostly dark frame, such as a lamp in a dim room or moonlight filtering through shadows. This technique, often used in night photography, requires precise light measurement to ensure that the light sources do not lose their detail while the surrounding areas contribute to the mood by remaining subdued.

By mastering the use of a light meter to measure and manipulate light precisely, photographers can extend beyond traditional exposure techniques. They can experiment with overexposure and underexposure to harness their full potential in storytelling and visual artistry. This not only broadens the scope of creative expression but also allows photographers to convey deeper narratives and emotions through their work.

In-Camera Light Metering

How to Use and Interpret In-Camera Metering

Understanding how to use and interpret in-camera metering is essential for photographers who wish to effectively manage exposure and capture images that are visually striking and technically sound. In-camera metering systems evaluate the light coming through the lens using a reflective light meter approach and automatically suggest camera settings that should yield a properly exposed photograph. This system's success hinges on the photographer's ability to select the appropriate metering mode and interpret the meter's reading accurately.

Modern cameras typically offer three primary metering modes: spot, center-weighted, and evaluative (sometimes called matrix or multi-segment metering). Each mode handles light measurement differently and serves different photographic needs. Spot metering measures a very small area of the scene, typically at the center or where the autofocus point is set. This mode is highly precise and ideal for situations where the subject is backlit or when there are high contrasts within the scene. It allows photographers to expose for the subject's key features without regard for the rest of the scene's lighting.

Center-weighted metering, on the other hand, evaluates the light in the middle of the frame while also considering the surrounding area but gives priority to the center. This mode is particularly useful for portraits or any photographs where the main subject is centrally located. The camera assumes that the subject is in the middle of the frame and thus should be the focal point of exposure.

Evaluative metering is more complex and analyzes the entire scene in zones to determine the best overall exposure. The camera evaluates multiple areas of the frame and considers factors such as color, luminance, focus, and even distance data if available from the autofocus system. This mode is highly versatile and suitable for most situations, particularly in evenly lit scenes.

To effectively use these metering modes, photographers must understand the scene's lighting dynamics and how different subjects might affect the metering. For instance, reflective surfaces or unusually dark or bright backgrounds can fool the metering system into underexposing or overexposing the image. Therefore, it is often necessary to adjust the recommended exposure settings based on the specific circumstances of the subject and environment.

Photographers should also familiarize themselves with their camera's exposure compensation feature, which allows for manual adjustment of the exposure suggested by the metering system.

This adjustment is crucial in scenarios where the metering system might be misled by elements within the frame. By experimenting with exposure compensation, photographers learn to override the camera's automatic settings when necessary to achieve the desired exposure level.

Understanding the histogram provided by most digital cameras can further aid photographers in interpreting in-camera metering. The histogram is a graphical representation of the tonal distribution in a photo, showing whether the image is generally well-exposed or if there are areas of underexposure (shown on the left side of the histogram) or overexposure (shown on the right side). By evaluating the histogram after taking a photograph, photographers can decide if they need to adjust their metering mode or exposure settings before taking another shot.

In summary, mastering in-camera metering involves selecting the right metering mode for the situation, understanding how to interpret the camera's meter readings, adjusting exposure settings as needed, and using tools like histograms to verify exposure accuracy. With practice and knowledge, photographers can harness in-camera metering to create consistently well-exposed images across a variety of lighting conditions.

Metering Modes: Spot, Center-Weighted, and Evaluative

In the realm of in-camera light metering, three primary modes—spot, center-weighted, and evaluative—play pivotal roles in helping photographers achieve the desired exposure for their images. Each mode offers a unique way of analyzing the light in the frame, catering to different photographic needs and scenarios.

Spot metering is highly precise, focusing on a very small area of the scene, typically about 1-5% of the viewfinder area at the center. This mode is particularly useful when the subject is backlit or when there are significant variations in light within the scene. Photographers often use spot metering to expose correctly for the subject's face in a portrait, ensuring that the facial features are neither overexposed nor underexposed, regardless of a brighter or darker background. This technique requires careful aim, as the metering is confined to such a small area.

Center-weighted metering takes a broader approach, evaluating the light in the middle of the frame while still giving priority to the central part of the image. Typically, this mode assumes that the subject is located in the center and thus prioritizes its exposure over the edges of the frame. It is a versatile mode, well-suited for portraits and other subjects that are centrally located. Center-weighted metering is less influenced by small areas of high contrast that might skew the exposure in spot metering mode, making it a good general-use option.

Evaluative metering, known in some camera systems as matrix or multi-segment metering, is the most complex and versatile of the metering modes. This mode analyzes the light in multiple zones across the entire frame, then combines these readings to determine the optimal exposure. The camera's processor uses a sophisticated algorithm that considers factors such as color, luminance, and focus distance, with particular attention to areas in focus, which is assumed to contain the main subject. Evaluative metering is particularly effective in handling scenes with complex lighting situations and is well-suited for dynamic environments like landscapes or scenes where the light and subjects are constantly changing.

Understanding when and how to switch between these metering modes allows photographers to respond to challenging lighting conditions more effectively. Spot metering is essential for capturing small, brightly lit subjects against dark backgrounds; center-weighted metering offers reliability for traditional portraits and everyday situations; and evaluative metering provides the sophisticated analysis needed for complex lighting and compositional scenarios. Mastering these tools empowers photographers to not just capture exposures accurately, but also creatively manipulate metering to enhance the artistic impact of their imagery.

Adjusting Exposure Compensation

Adjusting exposure compensation is a fundamental technique for photographers aiming to achieve the perfect exposure in their images, especially when relying on a camera's built-in light metering system. The in-camera light meter is designed to evaluate the light in a scene and suggest the best settings to achieve what it interprets as a correct exposure based on the reflectivity of the scene. However, these meters can be deceived by very bright or very dark subjects or backgrounds, leading to photos that are too bright or too dark. Exposure compensation allows the photographer to override the camera's automatic settings to better suit the specific needs of the subject or the artistic intent of the photographer.

Exposure compensation is typically adjustable via a dedicated dial or through the camera's menu system. It's measured in stops of light, with each stop representing a doubling or halving of the amount of light the camera allows in. The scale commonly ranges from -3 to +3 stops, though some cameras may offer a wider range. Adjusting the exposure compensation is like telling the camera to interpret the metered light differently. For example, if a scene contains predominantly bright tones, the camera might underexpose the shot, thinking it is letting in too much light; dialing in positive exposure compensation will correct this by making the image brighter.

Understanding when and how much exposure compensation to apply requires some knowledge and experience with how different conditions affect the light meter's reading. For scenes with high contrast, where there's a significant difference between the lightest and darkest parts of the scene, photographers might find themselves frequently adjusting the compensation to prevent losing detail in shadows or highlights. In snowy conditions or on bright sandy beaches, positive compensation can help overcome the camera's tendency to underexpose such predominantly white scenes. Conversely, in a dark forest or at a nighttime event, negative compensation might be necessary to prevent the camera from overexposing the scene in its attempt to make a dark scene appear artificially light.

To effectively use exposure compensation, it's also essential to understand the metering modes available on the camera. Most cameras offer several, including spot, center-weighted, and matrix or evaluative metering. Each of these modes dictates how the camera measures the light of a scene and thus influences the adjustments needed:

- **Spot metering** measures light in a very small area of the frame, which is great for scenes where the subject is significantly brighter or darker than the background.
- **Center-weighted metering** gives priority to the center of the frame and is typically used for portraits where the subject is centrally located.

- **Matrix or evaluative metering** analyzes the entire scene to determine the best overall exposure, making it useful for general photography and complex lighting situations.

Utilizing exposure compensation effectively requires a good understanding of how different lighting conditions affect the scene and a clear intention for how the final image should appear. By mastering this tool, photographers can ensure their images match their vision, despite the camera's automatic metering decisions. This level of control is crucial for both amateur and professional photographers alike as it allows for greater creativity and precision in photography.

Using Light Meters in Different Genres of Photography

Portrait Photography

Portrait photography is a genre that demands precision in capturing the subtleties of expression, mood, and character, making the mastery of light crucial. Using a light meter effectively within this genre ensures that the photographer can achieve the desired emphasis on the subject while maintaining detail and avoiding harsh shadows or overexposed highlights.

In portrait photography, light meters help to create a balance between ambient light and artificial lighting setups. The choice between using an incident or reflective light meter plays a significant role in how these elements are balanced. An incident light meter is particularly useful in studio settings or controlled lighting environments. It measures the light falling on the subject, rather than the light reflected by it, which is essential for capturing true skin tones without the influence of their color or the reflectiveness of their clothing.

By placing the incident meter close to the subject's face and pointing it toward the camera, the photographer can determine the optimal exposure settings that reflect the subject's true luminance. This method avoids the common pitfalls of underexposure or overexposure that can occur with highly reflective accessories or certain skin tones. For example, when photographing a subject with very light skin, a reflective meter might read too much light and suggest settings that would underexpose the shot. Conversely, for a subject with dark skin, it might indicate insufficient light and lead to overexposure. The incident light meter sidesteps these issues, providing a direct read of the light's impact on the subject.

Reflective light meters, typically built into cameras, are also used in portrait photography, especially in more dynamic or natural environments where the lighting cannot be controlled as easily. When using a reflective meter, the photographer must be mindful of its tendency to be influenced by the dominant tones in the frame. This can be particularly challenging in portraiture if the background is significantly brighter or darker than the subject, or if the subject wears highly reflective or absorptive materials. To counteract potential discrepancies, photographers often take multiple readings at different points around the subject's face and attire, using an averaging method to set the camera's exposure. This approach helps in achieving a more balanced exposure that enhances the subject's features.

Moreover, mastering the use of a light meter in portrait photography involves understanding the light quality, not just its intensity. Soft, diffused light often works best for portraits as it reduces the appearance of blemishes and provides a more flattering light on the face. A light meter can assist in adjusting the settings on diffusers or reflectors to achieve this quality of light, whether in a studio with artificial lights or outdoors using natural light.

In summary, effective use of light meters in portrait photography involves choosing the right type of meter for the lighting conditions and understanding how to interpret its readings accurately. Whether in a controlled studio setting using an incident light meter to capture nuanced exposures, or on location with a reflective meter managing dynamic light sources, the careful application of these tools allows photographers to elevate their portrait work, ensuring each photograph renders the subject in the most compelling and visually appealing manner.

Landscape Photography

Landscape photography captures the breadth and depth of nature and our surroundings, often requiring a deep understanding of light to convey the true essence of a scene. Using a light meter in landscape photography can dramatically improve the precision of exposures, particularly in environments where lighting conditions change rapidly, such as during sunrise or sunset.

When engaging in landscape photography, the primary challenge is managing the extreme range of light that can vary from the darkest shadows to the brightest highlights. A light meter becomes an invaluable tool here, helping photographers achieve a balanced exposure that captures the details in both areas without losing information.

For many landscape photographers, a reflective light meter, typically built into the camera, is the starting point for measuring light. This type of metering allows photographers to assess the brightness of different elements within the frame directly through the lens. By using the spot metering mode, which is a feature of many reflective meters, photographers can measure specific areas of a scene, allowing for adjustments based on precise, localized readings. This is particularly useful in landscape photography where the sky might be significantly brighter than the earth or where shadows cast by mountains require careful exposure to capture detailed textures.

However, there are scenarios in landscape photography where an incident light meter might be advantageous. For example, in pre-visualization stages or when setting up for a shot during the golden hour, an incident meter can help determine the overall exposure needed without being misled by the brightness of the sky or reflective surfaces like water. This approach involves measuring the light falling on the scene from the direction of the camera, ensuring that the exposure is not influenced by the scene's reflectivity, which is a common challenge when relying solely on the camera's built-in meter.

Additionally, the use of light meters in landscape photography is not just about achieving technical accuracy but also about artistic expression. For instance, understanding how to manipulate exposure can help create mood and atmosphere. Overexposing slightly can convey a hazy, ethereal scene, while underexposing can enhance colors and shadows, adding drama. Advanced light meters that offer features like high dynamic range (HDR) metering can guide photographers in capturing wider ranges of light, allowing for post-processing techniques that bring out maximum detail in both shadows and highlights.

Moreover, landscape photographers often face environmental factors such as fog, mist, or reflective light from snow and water. Each of these conditions can trick a camera's reflective meter into underexposing or overexposing the photograph. Here, a handheld light meter can be particularly useful for taking readings in different parts of the scene to determine the optimal average exposure settings, thus compensating for the camera meter's potential biases.

By integrating a light meter into their workflow, landscape photographers not only refine their technique but also deepen their connection with the natural world, translating fleeting moments of natural beauty into compelling, well-exposed images that resonate with viewers. The skillful use of a light meter in landscape photography ensures that the photographer can reliably capture the dynamic and often unpredictable lighting of outdoor environments, transforming them into stunning photographic art.

Street Photography

Street photography captures the spontaneity and candid moments of everyday life in urban environments. It requires a blend of quick reflexes, keen observation, and technical skills, one of which includes the adept use of a light meter. Understanding and utilizing a light meter in street photography can significantly enhance the quality and impact of the images captured.

In street photography, light conditions can change rapidly, influenced by factors such as the movement of the sun, shifting shadows, reflections from buildings, or even the sudden contrast between brightly lit areas and dark alleys. Here, both incident and reflective light meters play pivotal roles in helping photographers manage these changing lighting conditions effectively.

Using an incident light meter helps street photographers to gauge the ambient light that illuminates the scene. This can be particularly useful during the golden hours—early morning or late afternoon—when the light is warm and changes tone quickly. By measuring the light falling around their immediate location, photographers can set their camera to expose the scene accurately before even lifting the camera to their eye. This proactive approach is beneficial for capturing fleeting moments with more accuracy in exposure, ensuring that the dynamic range within the scene is maintained without losing detail in both shadows and highlights.

Reflective light meters, typically built into cameras, are more commonly used in street photography due to their convenience and speed. When pointing the camera at a scene, the reflective light meter evaluates the brightness of different elements, from which it calculates the exposure. However, this type of metering can be tricky in street photography because it can easily be fooled by unexpected reflections or unusually dark or light surfaces. It is crucial for photographers to understand this and possibly adjust the exposure compensation on their camera accordingly. For example, if a scene includes a large bright wall or a dark shadowed area, the meter might misread the light and either overexpose or underexpose the image. Learning how to quickly adjust the settings based on the meter's reading, often by relying on experience and instinct, is a key skill in street photography.

Moreover, street photographers often utilize a technique known as 'zone focusing'—setting a fixed aperture and focus distance—allowing them to shoot without having to re-meter and refocus for each shot. This method works well with a pre-determined understanding of light levels, which can be initially measured using a light meter. Once the general exposure settings are established, photographers can concentrate on composition and capturing the moment as it unfolds, rather than being distracted by technical adjustments.

Finally, understanding the nuances of light in different urban environments allows street photographers to use their light meters not just for technical accuracy but as tools for creative expression. They can play with shadows, silhouettes, backlighting, and highlights to create mood, depth, and emotion in their photos. A light meter becomes not just a device for measuring light but a guide that aids in translating the visual drama of street life into compelling photographic narratives.

In conclusion, effectively using a light meter in street photography involves more than simply achieving the correct exposure; it's about understanding and manipulating light to convey the essence of the urban landscape. Whether using incident or reflective meters, the key lies in how well a photographer can adapt their techniques to capture the ephemeral and vibrant scenes that street photography is known for.

Studio Photography

Studio photography is a domain where precision in lighting is paramount, and the effective use of light meters plays a crucial role in achieving this precision. In a controlled environment like a studio, photographers have the ability to manipulate lighting to create a desired effect or mood, making the accurate measurement of light essential to ensure the subject is perfectly illuminated.

In studio settings, both incident and reflective light meters are utilized, each serving specific purposes that enhance the photographer's ability to capture high-quality images. An incident light meter is particularly valuable in studio photography because it measures the intensity of light falling directly on the subject. This type of metering is unaffected by the color or texture of the subject, which is beneficial when shooting a wide variety of subjects in terms of skin tones, clothing, or props. By measuring the light that actually reaches the subject, photographers can adjust their lights to ensure even and desired exposure levels throughout the image.

Using an incident light meter typically involves placing the meter where the subject is positioned and pointing it back towards the camera or the primary light source. This helps in determining the optimal settings for the camera's aperture and shutter speed, ensuring that the lighting setup complements the artistic vision. For example, in portrait photography within a studio, controlling the key light to sculpt the subject's features while maintaining sufficient fill light to avoid harsh shadows is crucial, and precise light metering aids in achieving this balance.

Reflective light meters, often built into cameras, are also used in studio photography, especially when dealing with complex setups or backgrounds. These meters assess the light bouncing off the subject and back to the camera, which can be helpful for checking the lighting ratio or contrast between different parts of a scene. For instance, when a backdrop needs to be lit differently than the subject to create depth or emphasize the subject, a reflective meter can provide the necessary readings to adjust the background lighting accordingly.

Moreover, light meters in a studio can help in crafting specific lighting setups, such as high key or low key lighting. High key lighting, which involves a lot of light to create a bright and uniformly lit scene, requires careful monitoring to avoid overexposure. Conversely, low key lighting, which uses minimal lighting to create moodier, shadow-rich images, needs precise control to ensure that the light is just right to capture the details in the shadows without losing them to underexposure.

Understanding how to effectively use a light meter in studio photography also involves familiarity with the different sync speeds of studio strobes and cameras, as well as the impact of different modifiers like umbrellas, softboxes, and grids on the quality and direction of light. The light meter helps ensure that all these elements work harmoniously to produce the intended photographic outcome.

In conclusion, mastery of light meters in studio photography not only involves knowing how to measure light accurately but also understanding how to interpret these measurements and apply them to one's creative vision. This ensures that the photographer can consistently produce technically sound and aesthetically pleasing photographs under varied and controlled lighting conditions.

Troubleshooting Common Issues

Addressing Inaccurate Readings

Addressing inaccurate readings from a light meter is a crucial step in ensuring that your photography achieves the desired exposure. Several factors can lead to these discrepancies, ranging from environmental conditions to technical malfunctions. Understanding how to troubleshoot and correct these inaccuracies is essential for any photographer looking to rely on their light meter as a dependable tool.

One common issue that leads to inaccurate readings is improper calibration of the light meter. Over time and with regular use, the accuracy of a light meter can drift. To address this, regularly calibrate your device according to the manufacturer's instructions. Some high-end light meters may require professional calibration services, while others can be adjusted using reference light sources or calibration frames available for purchase.

Another challenge arises from environmental factors such as extreme lighting conditions. For instance, very bright or very dark environments can push a light meter beyond its operational limits. In these scenarios, it's beneficial to cross-verify meter readings with a different type of meter or adjust the meter's settings if it has options to handle such extremes. Additionally, using a light meter in indirect or mixed lighting conditions can result in flawed readings due to the meter being unable to distinguish between light sources. In such cases, consider using manual spot metering to focus on key areas of the scene, ensuring that the most important elements are correctly exposed.

Incorrect use of the meter itself can also lead to problems. For example, not correctly setting the ISO or the metering mode to match the scene being photographed can skew results. Ensure that you double-check these settings before taking a reading. It's also crucial to understand the difference between incident and reflective metering modes, as choosing the wrong one can affect the exposure dramatically. Reflective metering can be especially problematic with subjects that are unusually light or dark, as the meter may misinterpret the amount of light actually available.

Additionally, the angle at which the meter is held can impact its accuracy. This is particularly true for incident light meters, which should be pointed toward the camera from the subject's position to accurately measure the light falling on the subject. If the meter is angled away from the direct path of the incoming light, it may not provide a correct reading.

When all else fails, it may be a sign of a hardware issue. If your light meter consistently gives erroneous readings despite troubleshooting, consider having it inspected by a professional.

Sometimes components like the sensor or the display might need repairs or replacement.

By methodically addressing these potential issues, you can minimize the occurrence of inaccurate readings. Regular practice in varied lighting conditions will also help you become more proficient in anticipating and adjusting for factors that could affect your light meter's accuracy. With these strategies, photographers can trust their light meter to be an invaluable ally in capturing perfectly exposed photographs.

Dealing with Low Light Conditions

Dealing with low light conditions is a common challenge for photographers, often leading to underexposed images and increased noise. However, with the right techniques and understanding of how to use a light meter, these issues can be effectively managed, ensuring clear, well-exposed photos even in less-than-ideal lighting.

When working in low light, the primary goal is to maximize the available light to achieve a balanced exposure without compromising on the shutter speed or image quality. A light meter can be invaluable here by providing accurate readings that guide your camera settings.

The first step in managing low light conditions with a light meter is to set your meter to its most sensitive ISO setting. This adjustment allows the meter to detect even minimal light, making it easier to evaluate the exposure needed. While higher ISO settings can introduce grain or noise into the image, modern cameras and noise reduction software can help mitigate these effects, making it a worthwhile trade-off for the increased sensitivity.

In addition to adjusting the ISO, it's crucial to use the light meter to experiment with different apertures and shutter speeds. In low light, a wider aperture (a lower f-number) lets more light into the lens, which can be especially helpful. The light meter will guide you on how wide you can go before the depth of field becomes too shallow for your subject. Similarly, a slower shutter speed allows more light to hit the sensor, which is beneficial in dim conditions. However, this can cause blurring from camera shake or subject movement. Here, a tripod and a remote shutter release can be essential tools to stabilize your camera and keep your images sharp.

Reflective light metering techniques often face difficulties in low light as the meter may struggle to accurately read the light reflecting off the subject. This is where switching to an incident light meter can be advantageous. An incident light meter doesn't rely on the light reflected by the subject; instead, it measures the light falling onto the subject, which typically provides a more accurate reading in dim environments.

When all else fails, bracketing exposures is a reliable method to ensure at least one suitable result. This technique involves taking multiple shots of the same scene at different exposure settings (as indicated by your light meter readings). Later, you can select the best-exposed image or even blend these images in post-processing for optimal results.

Furthermore, understanding the behavior of light in low light conditions can significantly enhance your use of the light meter. Soft, diffused light sources often provide better illumination for low light photography, reducing the contrast and softening shadows that harsh light might exacerbate. Positioning your subject closer to these light sources can also maximize the light's effectiveness.

By mastering the use of a light meter in low light conditions, photographers can overcome the challenges posed by inadequate lighting. This ensures the capture of striking images with good exposure, bringing out the details and mood of the scene without succumbing to the pitfalls of noise and blur. Thus, a light meter not only serves as a technical tool but also as a companion in exploring the creative potential that low light photography offers.

Tips for Maintaining Your Light Meter

Maintaining your light meter is crucial for ensuring its accuracy and longevity, whether it's a handheld device or built into your camera. Proper care involves regular checks, careful handling, and an understanding of common issues that might arise. Here's a comprehensive guide to keeping your light meter in top condition and troubleshooting typical problems.

Regular Calibration: Light meters should be calibrated regularly to ensure accuracy. This is particularly important for professional photographers who depend on precise exposure readings. Calibration involves comparing the meter's readings with a known light source or another calibrated meter. This process can sometimes require professional servicing, especially for older or heavily used meters.

Battery Care: For handheld meters, battery health is vital. Always ensure that the battery is charged and functioning well. Low battery power can lead to inaccurate readings. It's wise to carry spare batteries and replace them periodically, even if they don't appear to be depleted. In the case of meters showing erratic behavior, the first step should be to check and possibly replace the battery.

Protect from Extreme Conditions: Light meters are sensitive to extreme environmental conditions. Avoid exposing your meter to excessive moisture, dust, or heat, as these can affect the meter's internal components. When using your meter in harsh conditions, protective cases or covers can help shield it from damage.

Handling and Storage: Physical damage is a common issue with light meters, especially handheld models. Handle your meter with care, avoiding drops or impacts. When not in use, store your meter in a padded case away from direct sunlight and extreme temperatures, which can warp or degrade the casing and internal components.

Cleanliness: Keep the light sensor and body of the meter clean. Dust, dirt, or smudges on the sensor can obstruct light and skew readings. Use a soft, dry cloth to clean the meter. For tougher spots or to clean the sensor area, use a blower or brush specifically designed for camera sensors and delicate electronics.

Firmware Updates: For newer digital meters and meters integrated within cameras, keeping the firmware up to date is important. Manufacturers may release updates to improve accuracy, compatibility, or functionality. Check the manufacturer's website regularly for updates and follow their instructions to install them.

Check for Consistency: Regularly check your meter's consistency by taking multiple readings under the same lighting conditions. Inconsistencies might indicate a problem with the meter or its settings. If readings fluctuate, refer to the troubleshooting section of your manual or contact the manufacturer for advice.

Professional Servicing: If your light meter is malfunctioning and you cannot resolve the issue through basic troubleshooting, professional servicing may be necessary. This is particularly true for complex issues like internal electronic faults or recalibration needs.

By following these maintenance tips, you can help ensure that your light meter remains a reliable tool for your photography, providing precise readings that allow you to capture beautifully exposed images consistently. Proper care not only extends the life of your light meter but also ensures it functions accurately, helping you achieve the best possible results in your photographic endeavors.

Case Studies and Practical Examples

Real-life Scenarios of Using a Light Meter

Understanding the real-life applications of a light meter can greatly enhance a photographer's ability to consistently achieve high-quality results. Various scenarios illustrate the effectiveness of using a light meter across different photography genres and conditions, revealing how critical this tool is in diverse situations.

In the realm of **portrait photography**, a light meter plays an invaluable role, particularly when working with complex lighting setups. Consider a professional photographer tasked with capturing a series of indoor family portraits. By using an incident light meter, the photographer can determine the exact amount of light each member of the family is receiving, especially in a setting where natural light from nearby windows interacts unpredictably with artificial studio lights. For example, if the light meter indicates that one side of the room is underexposed, the photographer can adjust additional lights accordingly to ensure even illumination, resulting in uniformly exposed images where all subjects are depicted clearly and vividly.

Landscape photography presents a different set of challenges, often requiring the use of a reflective light meter built into the camera. A landscape photographer might find themselves at a scenic overlook, capturing the sunset over a mountain range. The varying luminance levels between the sky and the land can create exposure discrepancies. Here, the photographer can use the spot metering mode of their camera's built-in light meter to measure specific areas—such as the brightest part of the sky and the darkest part of the mountain—and then average these readings to set an exposure that maintains detail in both the highlights and shadows. This technique allows for capturing a balanced image that reflects more accurately the natural beauty of the scene.

In the context of **event photography**, which often involves rapidly changing lighting conditions, the ability to quickly measure and adjust to different lighting situations is crucial. A photographer covering a live music event, for example, faces the challenge of dramatic lighting changes as spotlights and stage effects shift throughout performances. Using a handheld light meter allows the photographer to quickly adjust camera settings on the fly, ensuring that the exposure is correct no matter how the stage lighting changes. This capability is vital for capturing the dynamic and vibrant nature of live performances without losing details to underexposure or overexposure.

Wedding photography also benefits significantly from the use of both types of light meters. During a wedding, a photographer might use an incident light meter for formal portraits to guarantee that the intricate details of the wedding dress are visible and not washed out by bright lighting. Conversely, a reflective light meter could be more suitable for capturing the ambiance of the reception where the lighting might be dimmer and more variable. The reflective meter helps ensure that the mood and setting are captured accurately, reflecting the intimate and festive atmosphere of the event.

These practical examples demonstrate how light meters can be essential tools in managing exposure across various types of photography. By understanding and utilizing both incident and reflective light meters appropriately, photographers enhance their ability to adapt to any lighting condition, thus improving the technical quality of their photos while also capturing their artistic vision.

Comparative Analysis of Metered vs. Non-metered Photographs

In the pursuit of photographic excellence, the use of light meters compared to relying on one's eye or automatic camera settings (non-metered approaches) can significantly impact the quality of images produced. Through practical examples and case studies, it becomes evident how metered photography offers precision and consistency that is often hard to achieve with non-metered methods.

Case Study 1: Landscape Photography
A photographer set out to capture the sunrise over a mountain range. Two shots were taken; one used a handheld light meter to measure the incident light at dawn, while the other relied on the camera's built-in metering system (reflective metering). The metered photograph had well-balanced exposure with clear details in both the brightly lit sky and the darker foreground. The non-metered photo, influenced by the bright sunrise, resulted in underexposed shadows where much of the detail was lost. The incident light meter helped the photographer adjust the exposure settings to capture a broader dynamic range, effectively showcasing the subtle hues and textures of the landscape.

Case Study 2: Portrait Photography in Studio
In this scenario, a portrait photographer used a light meter to set up her studio lighting for a series of headshots. By measuring the

light falling on different areas of the subject's face, the photographer was able to achieve a soft, evenly distributed light, avoiding harsh shadows or overexposure often seen in portraits. Conversely, another set of headshots taken without a light meter resulted in less consistent lighting, with some shots showing overblown highlights and others appearing too dim. The precision provided by the light meter ensured that the lighting setup was optimal for capturing detailed, flattering portraits.

Practical Example: Wedding Photography
During a wedding, a photographer alternated between using a light meter for critical shots and relying on the camera's auto-exposure for more candid moments. The metered photographs of the ceremony, specifically during the exchange of vows under a canopy, displayed excellent exposure with the couple well-highlighted against a softly lit background. In contrast, the non-metered shots captured during the reception had varying quality, with some images overexposed due to the complex lighting environment of the venue, including string lights and bright windows.

Practical Example: Street Photography
A street photographer conducting an experiment used a reflective light meter built into the camera for some images and an incident light meter for others. The photos taken with the incident light meter consistently showed better exposure. The reflective metering often misread scenes with high contrast, like a dark

alleyway with a bright exit, leading to poorly exposed subjects. The incident meter's readings, on the other hand, allowed the photographer to manually adjust settings that accounted for the actual amount of light available, capturing more detail and mood of the street scenes.

These case studies and examples illustrate that while non-metered photography can yield good results in conditions with consistent or predictable lighting, metered photography provides a clear advantage in challenging lighting conditions or when precision is necessary. Using a light meter, photographers can make informed decisions about exposure, leading to higher quality photographs that are true to the photographer's vision. This comparative analysis clearly shows the benefits of using a light meter, advocating for its essential role in the toolkit of serious photographers who demand control and consistency in their work.

Conclusion

The insights gathered from mastering the use of a light meter prove invaluable across all forms of photography, from amateur shoots in the backyard to professional studio settings. The ability to measure light accurately not only elevates the technical quality of images but also enhances the photographer's understanding of how light interacts with subjects in various environments.

Utilizing a light meter allows photographers to make more informed decisions about exposure settings, leading to images that are not only technically sound but also aesthetically pleasing. Whether it's capturing the subtle gradations in a sunset or ensuring that a model's skin tone is flawlessly depicted, a light meter provides the data necessary to achieve the desired result. This accuracy is particularly crucial in scenarios where lighting conditions are complex or changing rapidly, and where camera auto-exposure systems often fall short.

Beyond mere exposure, the knowledge and application of light metering contribute to a photographer's ability to convey mood and atmosphere. The intentional overexposure for a dreamy, washed-out effect or underexposure to create mood and mystery can be executed with precision when the exact light levels are known. In essence, light meters empower photographers to transform their vision into reality meticulously.

Moreover, the consistent use of a light meter cultivates a discipline in photographers that transcends the technical aspects of the craft. It encourages a systematic approach to shooting that can significantly improve workflow and output quality. Photographers find that with regular use, they can predict exposure settings even before metering the light, enhancing their efficiency and confidence.

In conclusion, investing time to understand and use a light meter effectively is more than learning another photographic technique. It is about embracing an essential tool that promises greater creative control, consistent results, and the ability to capture images that resonate with clarity and depth. The advantages of using a light meter, as outlined through various practical applications, underscore its indispensability for anyone serious about photography, making it clear why it should be an integral part of every photographer's toolkit.

www.ingramcontent.com/pod-product-compliance
Lightning Source LLC
Chambersburg PA
CBHW050327230526
45471CB00005B/2379